THE
HEART
SPEAKS...

THE
HEART
SPEAKS...

CREATING
YOUR OWN
HEAVEN
ON
EARTH

BY
MARILYN SEGAL

Published by Twin-Lynn Inc. Atlanta, Georgia.
Printed in the United States of America.

5 4 3 2 1

Cover art, illustrations, and text lettering by Marilyn Segal
Edited by Phyllis Mueller
Cover design by Kathy Couch
Printing coordination by Daly Graphics, Inc.
Author's photo by George Eckard

For additional copies or information about workshops by Marilyn Segal, please write:
Twin-Lynn Inc.
1180 Branch Water Court
Atlanta, Georgia 30338

INTRODUCTION AND SPECIAL THANKS

THIS BOOK BEGAN BECAUSE I WANTED TO GIVE MY FATHER, BOB, A SPECIAL GIFT MONEY COULDN'T BUY. I STARTED BY WRITING THOUGHTS THAT CAME TO ME AS I READ AND EXPERIENCED MY OWN SPIRITUAL GROWTH, AND THEN PUT DRAWINGS WITH MY THOUGHTS. ONE THOUGHT LED TO ANOTHER, AND AS I BEGAN HELPING OTHERS, THE BOOK GREW.

♡ I THANK MY NIECE, CARLY, FOR SHARING WITH ME HER STRUGGLES IN TRYING TO COMMUNICATE WITH HER MOTHER.

♡ I THANK IVY BLUM FOR HELPING ME SEE THE OTHER SIDE OF LOSING A LOVED ONE. I LOST MY MOTHER WHEN I WAS ELEVEN, AND IT HELPED ME WHEN IVY SHARED HER OWN FEELINGS ABOUT LEAVING HER CHILDREN AND NOT SEEING THEM GROW. MAY SHE REST IN PEACE.

♡ I THANK MY FAMILY, FRIENDS, CLIENTS, AND EMPLOYERS WHO HAVE MIRRORED INTO ME WHAT I NEEDED TO HEAL IN ORDER TO GROW. APPRECIATION AND LOVE TO ALL.

♡ I THANK MY DOG, SAMANTHA, WHO HAS BROUGHT TO MY LIFE A LOVE I NEVER EXPERIENCED.

♡ I THANK MY EDITOR, PHYLLIS MUELLER, WHO HAS BECOME A VERY DEAR PERSON IN MY LIFE. WITHOUT HER GUIDANCE, CONTRIBUTIONS, SUGGESTIONS, AND HELP, ALL THIS WOULD STILL BE PAGES IN A FOLDER.

♡ TO GERALD DALY, FOR ORCHESTRATING THE DETAILS AND GETTING THIS BOOK TO PRINT.

♡ TO MY WONDERFUL HUSBAND TERRY, WHO HAS LOVED ME AND BELIEVED IN ME THROUGHOUT OUR YEARS OF MARRIAGE. HE HAS BEEN MY ROCK; WITH HIS SUPPORT I GAINED

STRENGTH TO SEARCH FOR MY TRUTHS
AND MY PURPOSE. "REMEMBER WHEN"
IS FOR YOU, TERRY. YOU HELPED ME
FIND MY OWN HEAVEN ON EARTH.
I LOVE YOU WITH ALL MY HEART.

♡ A SPECIAL THANKS TO GOD AND MY
GUARDIAN ANGELS, WHO CONTINUE TO
GUIDE AND WATCH OVER ME.

BLESS YOU ALL !!!

CONTENTS

REMEMBER...

REMEMBER WHEN YOU
WERE A KID, AND PLAY
WAS A FULL-TIME JOB...
AND YOU NEEDED TO EAT
TO FILL YOUR BODY WITH
ENOUGH FUEL TO KEEP GOING,

REMEMBER WHEN ...

FROGS AND SPIDERS AND LIZARDS WERE YOUR FRIENDS?

REMEMBER WHEN...

YOUR IMAGINARY FRIENDS
WOULD COME AND PLAY
WITH YOU

AND

ENTERTAIN YOU

AND

BE WITH YOU
ALWAYS!?

LIFE WAS SIMPLE,
KIND,
AND
NEVER SCARY,

REMEMBER THE LONG
DRIVE TO THE BEACH
WHEN YOU ALWAYS
WANTED TO KNOW...

'ARE WE
   THERE YET?'

AND THE ENDLESS HUNT
FOR THE MOST INCREDIBLE
SEASHELLS?

AND THE WAVES THAT
POUNDED THE SAND?

AND THE AIR THAT WAS SO THICK YOU FELT BUGS WOULD STICK TO YOUR SKIN?

REMEMBER WHEN LIFE WAS SO SIMPLE AND WE WERE SO CAREFREE?

REMEMBER WHEN THE
WINTER DAYS WERE SO
SHORT AND SO COLD,
AND THE SNOW PILED SO
HIGH, AND THE SLEDS
COVERED THE HILLSIDE,

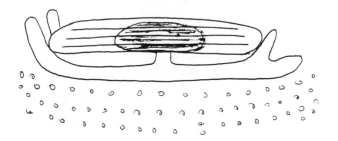

AND THERE WOULD BE
SNOWBALL FIGHTS?

AND you WOULD BE
BUNDLED UP SO TIGHT IN ALL
THE CLOTHES THAT WOULD
FIT ONTO YOUR LITTLE BODY
TO KEEP YOU WARM...

BUT DRY?? THAT
WAS
SOMETHING
ELSE,

AND AFTER A LONG HARD
PLAY IN THE SNOW, YOU
WOULD COME INTO A WARM
HOUSE AND THERE WOULD
BE A CUP OF HOT CHOCOLATE
WAITING JUST
FOR YOU,

Miss
Beth

13

AND REMEMBER AFTER
THE COLD WINTERS WHEN
THE TREES WOULD START
TO BLOOM

AND

THE

FLOWERS

WOULD COME BACK
AFTER A LONG WINTER'S
NAP?

14

AND YOU'D FIND A
NEST FILLED WITH
BABY BIRDS BEING FED
BY THEIR MAMMA BIRD,

THOSE WERE THE DAYS!

15

AND REMEMBER WHEN
SUMMER DAYS WERE LONG
AND THE SKIES WERE BLUE

AND YOU COULD TAKE
ALL DAY TO EXPLORE NEW
TERRITORIES LIKE:
HAUNTED HOUSES
QUIET WOODS___

WHERE THE PLANTS AND
THE TREES WERE YOUR
FRIENDS

OR

AN OLD ABANDONED

MILL,

AND REMEMBER WHEN
THE LEAVES WOULD FALL
AND YOU WOULD RAKE THEM
INTO PILES ...
   JUST FOR JUMPING INTO?

THOSE WERE
   THE DAYS!

LIFE WAS <u>SO</u> EXCITING,
SO FILLED WITH JOY,
SO FILLED WITH
AMAZEMENT,
SO FILLED WITH THE
LOVE OF LIVING,

WHAT HAPPENED?

WHAT HAPPENED TO THAT
CHILD'S LIFE?

WHERE DID WE LOSE THE
WONDER?

WHERE DID WE LOSE THE FUN?

WHAT HAPPENED
TO THAT CHILD?

Was it just growing up?

Or could it be as
simple as a change
in our perception?

Can we touch that
child again?

ARE WE STILL THAT
SAME PERSON, BUT
ALL GROWN UP?

WE KNEW AS CHILDREN
HOW TO   LOVE - - -

WE LEARNED IT FROM

WONDERMENT, EXPERIENCE,

AND JOY IN LIVING;

BUT AS GROWN-UPS,
SOMEHOW WE HAVE

FORGOTTEN,

WE HAVE FORGOTTEN
BECAUSE WE HAVE "OTHER"
PRIORITIES,

BUT WHAT IS MORE
IMPORTANT?

LOVE OR

  "OTHER" PRIORITIES?

Sadly, as grownups,
our choice is often
those "other" things,
BECAUSE IT'S PART OF
THE PROCESS OF LEARNING
TO FIND OUT JUST HOW
IMPORTANT IT IS TO
<u>SET</u> AND <u>GET</u> OUR
PRIORITIES IN ORDER,

AND MAYBE AFTER THE
ROAD TO "OTHER" THINGS
LEADS YOU TO LONELINESS...

MAYBE THEN, YOUR PRIORITIES
WILL CHANGE,

MAYBE THEN YOU WILL
FOCUS ON LOVE,

AND HOW MIGHT YOU
DO THAT?

IF YOU CAN, LET THE SUN
WAKE YOU UP EACH MORNING,
LET GOD SAY HELLO FIRST,
FEEL HIS LIGHT UPON YOUR
FACE, WAKING YOU UP...

WAKING UP YOUR THOUGHTS,

HELLO

HELLO

HELLO

HELLO

27

WAKE UP EACH DAY WITH

A SMILE ON YOUR FACE,

AND WAKE UP WITH THE THOUGHT

"THIS IS THE BEST!"

AND FROM
THAT MOMENT ON...
LET THIS BE THE
BEST
DAY
EVER!!!

WHEN YOU ARE STUCK
OR DEPRESSED
OR FRUSTRATED
AND FEEL LIKE
CRYING...

Give yourself
PERMISSION TO RECOGNIZE
YOUR FEELINGS AND A
GREAT BIG PAT
ON THE BACK
FOR
ALLOWING
YOURSELF TO

FEEL

THESE VERY IMPORTANT
EMOTIONS,

34

It's time to stop holding back your tears and pushing your emotions under the rug,

FRUSTRATION

ANXIETY

SADNESS

FEAR

WITHOUT THESE EMOTIONS
YOU WOULD NEVER
GROW,
AND
WITHOUT
GROWING,
FRUSTRATION
NEVER ENDS,

It's time to find
out WHY

you're eating more
than you need

drinking to excess

shopping until you drop

watching T.V. all
day long,

37

These are ways we
hide our emotions
from others

And

especially from
Ourselves!

38

WE CAN CHOOSE TO
CONTINUE TO WALK IN
DARKNESS OR
WE CAN
TURN ON
OUR OWN

INNER LIGHT

TO FIND

OUR HAPPINESS
OUR TRUTHS
OUR PURPOSE,

BUT HOW?

IT'S ALL SO OVERWHELMING,

|st

THE FIRST STEP IS RESPONDING TO YOUR FEELINGS,

If you FEEL LIKE CRYING,
LET YOUR TEARS FLOW...
FOR TEARS
ARE HEALING,

AND AFTER THE TEARS IF
YOU FEEL LIKE SLEEPING--
SLEEP,
FOR SLEEP IS A WAY OF
HEALING TOO,

AND

IF YOU FEEL LIKE HAVING
YOUR FAVORITE TREAT
FROM WHEN YOU
WERE A KID...

HAVE IT,

AND HEAL THAT CHILD,

NURTURING YOURSELF
IS HEALING,

THE BIGGEST STEP IS
RECOGNIZING YOUR EMOTIONS
AND BEING ABLE TO
RESPOND WITH A NEW
POSITIVE BEHAVIOR,

AND ANYTHING
IN EXCESS IS
NOT POSITIVE,

AFTER YOU HAVE ALLOWED
YOUR TEARS TO FLOW AND
YOUR HEAD FEELS
    MUCH CLEARER
    (MUCH LIGHTER)
AND YOU'VE RESTED
AND NURTURED YOURSELF,
PLAN TO BE HAPPY,

MAKING A "HAPPY" LIST
CAN HELP.

SIT DOWN AND
WRITE ON PAPER
THINGS THAT
MAKE YOU
          HAPPY,

AND DO THEM.

IF YOU LIKE WATCHING
PEOPLE --- GO TO THE PARK
AND WATCH THE PEOPLE,

BEING OUTDOORS WITH
MOTHER NATURE MAY BE
JUST THE MEDICINE YOU
NEED,

IF YOU LIKE LISTENING
TO MUSIC --
FIND A
PLACE
THAT
PLAYS YOUR
TYPE OF
MUSIC
AND GO,
GET OUT AND ENJOY YOURSELF,

AND, IF REMEMBERING
YOURSELF
PLAYING
PUTT - PUTT
PUTS A SMILE
ON YOUR FACE --

GO PLAY,
GO AND HAVE FUN!
GIVE YOURSELF PERMISSION
TO HAVE FUN AND BE
HAPPY,

It's all in the
Doing!

If today passes you by,

There's always

Tomorrow,

FOR EACH DAY IS THE
CHANCE TO BEGIN AGAIN,

IT'S GOD'S GIFT TO
START EACH AND EVERY
DAY FRESH AND ALIVE,

BUT, IF YOU FIND
YOURSELF REPEATING
THE DAY BEFORE,

GIVE THANKS --

FOR GOD HAS GIVEN
YOU ANOTHER CHANCE
TO CHANGE AND

BE HAPPY!

You can talk "AT"
   SOMEONE,
You can talk "AROUND"
   SOMEONE,
You can talk "THROUGH"
   SOMEONE,

OR...
You can talk "WITH"
   SOMEONE,

You know what it
feels like when
someone talks "at" you,

You know what it
feels like when
someone talks "around" you,
AND
You know what it
feels like when
someone talks "through" you,

BUT WHAT DOES IT
FEEL LIKE WHEN SOMEONE
TALKS "WITH" YOU?

DO YOU FEEL SPECIAL?

YEAH!
YEAH!

... LIKE YOU ARE
ON TOP OF
THE WORLD?

Do you feel so connected to that person or that moment that you NEVER want it to stop?

Do you FEEL LIKE
SMILING AND SMILING
UNTIL
YOUR FACE STARTS TO HURT?

THIS IS THE BEGINNING OF THE MOST

INCREDIBLE

FORM OF ART,

THE ART OF
COMMUNICATION...

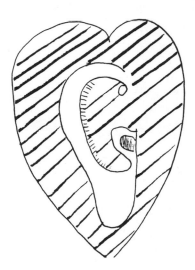

WHEN SOMEONE
TALKS WITH
YOU, YOU ARE
THERE <u>IN</u> THAT
MOMENT AND
LISTENING WITH
YOUR HEART,

63

HEARING WHAT THAT PERSON HAS TO SAY,

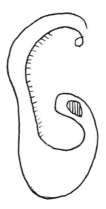

COMMUNICATION DOESN'T
ALWAYS NEED TO BE SPOKEN,

YOU CAN LISTEN WITH A
GESTURE, OR
A SMALL TOKEN OF
APPRECIATION, OR
A SMILE,

But what if someone tries to communicate with a loud voice... or with unkind words... or in a harsh tone...

Defenses go up, and the other person  stops listening,

AND

THE COMMUNICATION IS
BROKEN,

AND

HARSH, UGLY
WORDS START
FLYING,

STOP

IMMEDIATELY, AND

LOVE...

HERE AND NOW

STARTING RIGHT HERE
AND RIGHT NOW!

Ask for forgiveness
from your friend and
from yourself,

Apologize to each other
for the harsh ugly
words that you spoke,

69

AND GIVE EACH OTHER

A HUG —

OR AT LEAST A

WARM SMILE,

This will bring
communication back into
harmony,

If you want to be close
to someone,
get closer to them...

THROUGH
KINDNESS
THROUGH
FORGIVENESS
THROUGH
LOVE,

B_E THERE AND LISTEN
WITH A WARM SMILE
AND UNDIVIDED
ATTENTION,

"THAT" IS THE ART OF
COMMUNICATION!

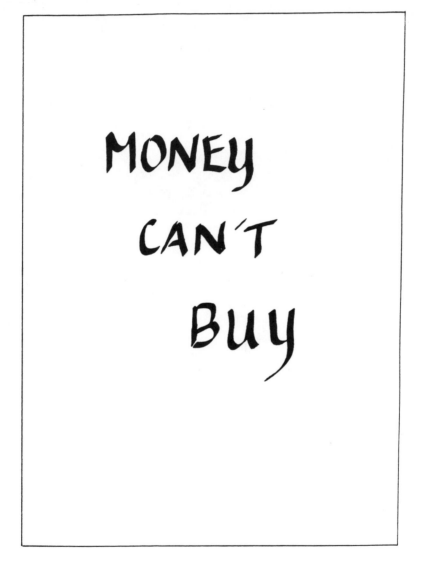

MONEY
CAN'T
BUY

I WANT TO GIVE YOU
SOMETHING MONEY
CAN'T BUY ...

A BOOK DEDICATED
AND WRITTEN
ESPECIALLY FOR YOU,

I PERSONALLY WOULD LOVE TO GIVE YOU THE GIFTS OF HAPPINESS, JOY AND PEACE OF MIND,

But those TREASURES
CAN ONLY BE FOUND
WITHIN YOU,

I CAN SHOW YOU THE
WAY TO BETTER HEALTH,

I WILL SHOW YOU WITH
OPEN ARMS
AND A SMILE,

THERE CAN BE NO PEACE
WHEN THERE IS CONFLICT,

THERE IS NO REASON TO
LEARN THROUGH PAIN,

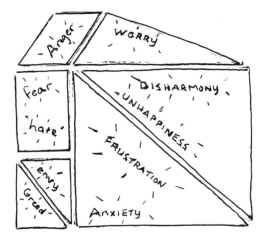

OUR THOUGHTS CAUSE PAIN, AND THESE THOUGHTS USUALLY SOUND LIKE THIS:

LIFE IS FUNNY, AND
LIFE HAS MANY PIECES
TO ITS PUZZLE,

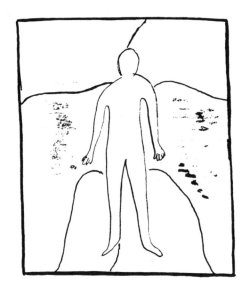

WITH THESE PIECES,
YOU HAVE FREE WILL,
AND YOU CAN CHOOSE
WHICH DIRECTION TO TAKE,

I CAN OFFER TOOLS
TO HELP YOU ALONG
THE WAY,

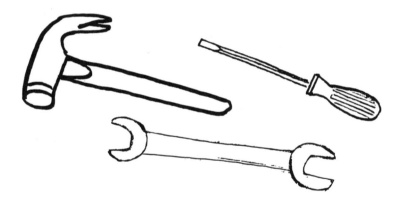

But my tool-box may
be different than most
other tool-boxes,

My tool-box contains
words and thoughts,

FORGIVING OTHERS AND
FORGIVING YOURSELF WILL
LEAD YOU TO

PEACE,

HAPPINESS,

LOVE &

JOY,

86

FORGIVENESS AND LOVE ARE
TWO IMPORTANT WORDS IN
THE HUMAN LANGUAGE,

UNFORTUNATE-LY THEY
ARE OFTEN FORGOTTEN,

In any situation,

Personal or professional,
we always can choose
how we react,

All too often, we get
caught up in our
reactions,

And that can be
quite ugly,

BUT ALL WE HAVE TO DO
IS THIS :
FORGIVE,

WE NEED TO FORGIVE
OURSELVES FOR REACTING
TO FEAR,

WHETHER THAT FEAR IS OF
CHANGE OR FEAR OF BEING
OUT OF CONTROL OF HOW THINGS
TURN OUT,

FEAR IS A CRY FOR LOVE,

It is no longer necessary
to fear,

Fear is heavy,

Joy is like love ...

LOVE AND JOY
ARE "LIGHT",

PART OF TEACHING IS TO
ENLIGHTEN YOURSELF,

LOVE FEELS LIGHT, NOT
HEAVY (LIKE WHEN YOU)
TENSE UP,

THE "LIGHT" IS ALREADY
WITHIN YOU,

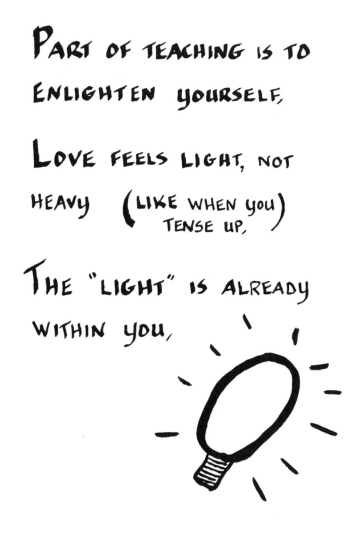

Suffering, at any time,
can be exchanged for Joy,

Recognition is the first
step to change,

Only you can take
that step,

THE NEXT STEP IS TO
CHANGE YOUR BEHAVIOR,
AND REACT WITH KINDNESS,

IF YOU PERCEIVE THE
WORLD AROUND YOU AS
LOVING AND KIND...

THAT WILL BE
THE WORLD YOU
WILL SEE,

94

FOR PERCEPTION IS OUR
MIRROR, AND OUR MIND
REFLECTS,

To teach is to learn
and
to learn is to teach,

Teach peace

Teach love

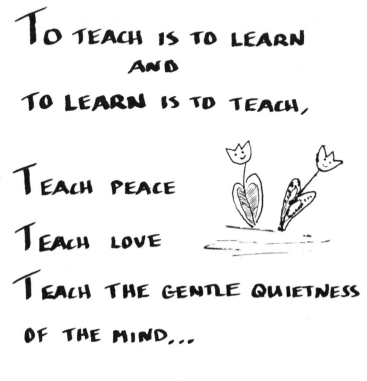

Teach the gentle quietness

of the mind...

That's where
you will find
Peace,

PRACTICE THIS AND IT WILL BE YOURS!!!

THIS IS MY GIFT OF HEALTH TO YOU,

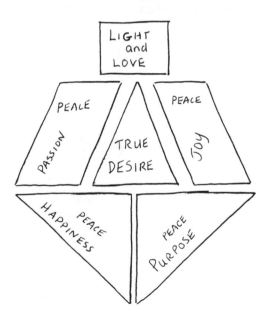

TURN ON THAT LIGHT
INSIDE AND INVITE IT TO
SHINE IN YOU, THROUGH YOU,
AND INTO OTHERS,

THE BEST GIFT I CAN GIVE YOU IS TO TEACH YOU LOVE,

I COULD HAVE BOUGHT YOU GOLF CLUBS, CARDS, CLOTHES, BUT...

I CHOSE TO GIVE YOU
THE GIFT OF LOVE,

BECAUSE NOTHING ELSE
MATTERS ...
BUT LOVE!

I WAS SO YOUNG...

AND MY MOTHER
WAS DYING,

BECAUSE I WAS SO
YOUNG
I HAD NOT LEARNED
HOW TO REACH OUT TO HER
AND TOUCH HER AND SAY
I LOVE YOU...

I WAS AFRAID
TO LISTEN

AFRAID
TO SHARE

AFRAID
TO CARE

AND AFRAID
TO LOVE,

BECAUSE I WAS AFRAID...

JUST PLAIN AFRAID,

Because what if:

I cared...

And

She died and went away?

And what if:

I shared...

My dreams

And

She died and went away?

And what if:
I loved...

And

She died and went away?

It REALLY HAPPENED,

SHE DID DIE

AND

SHE DID GO

AWAY BUT

BECAUSE

I WAS

AFRAID...

I DIDN'T SHARE
AND
   DIDN'T CARE
AND
   DIDN'T LOVE

EXCEPT FROM
A DISTANCE,

It TOOK ME YEARS
OF PAIN TO LEARN
WHAT I NEEDED
TO LEARN AS I WATCHED
MY MOTHER DIE,

I LEARNED IT IS
OKAY TO TALK ABOUT
FEELINGS ...

HERS AND MINE,

I LEARNED IT IS OKAY
TO BE AFRAID,

I LEARNED IT'S OKAY
TO REACH OUT AND
GIVE A HUG
AND TO STROKE A
DYING PERSON'S HAND,

I LEARNED IT'S OKAY
TO CRY AND BE SAD THAT
THIS SPECIAL PERSON
WOULD SOME DAY NO
LONGER BE WITH ME,

I LEARNED THAT ALL
THAT MATTERS IS
How WE
LOVE AND SHARE
AND CARE
RIGHT IN THIS MOMENT,

I LEARNED THAT
THIS WAS THE BEST
AND ONLY

PRESENT

I COULD GIVE HER,

LOVING
IN THE
PRESENT.

P.S. I LOVE YOU MOM

P. P.S. AND WHAT ABOUT ME?

I LEARNED I'M
OKAY!

RESPONSIBILITY

AND

COMMITMENT =

PROSPERITY

AND

HAPPINESS

RESPONSIBILITY...

THE ABILITY TO RESPOND,

THE ABILITY TO RESPOND
IN ANY GIVEN MOMENT,

THE ACTION BEHIND THE
WORD IS REALLY WHAT
COUNTS,

NOT HAVING RESPONSIBILITY

FREEZES UP YOUR THOUGHTS,

IT FREEZES UP YOUR ACTIONS,

AND

IT FREEZES UP YOUR LOVE,

124

You BECOME CONSUMED
BY YOUR MENTAL THOUGHTS
AND
YOU BECOME WORRIED
ABOUT YOUR EXTERNAL
WORLD,

WORRIES

THOSE
WORRIES
YOU PUT
OUT --
COME BACK TO YOU,

You FREEZE UP YOUR
BODY AND YOU CAN'T

MOVE FORWARD

IN YOUR

LIFE——

WITH

A RELATIONSHIP,

A JOB

OR PERSONAL

GROWTH,

RESPONSIBILITY HAS A

TWIN SISTER:

COMMITMENT— TO YOURSELF
AND TO OTHERS, THE FEAR
OF COMMITMENT LIVES IN THE
SHADOWS OF RESPONSIBILITY,

127

Commitment enables
you to respond.

If you fear
    Commitment,
you fear your responses
and you fear
    Responsibility.

THESE TWIN SISTERS,
RESPONSIBILITY
       AND
COMMITMENT, MUST LIVE
IN BALANCE AND
     HARMONY,

         BUT HOW?

THE FIRST STEP IS RECOGNIZING YOUR TRUTHS,

HEAR THE WORDS YOU THINK,

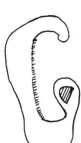

ARE THE WORDS YOU THINK AND SPEAK OUT OF LOVE?

HEAR THE WORDS YOU SPEAK,

130

If you constantly
say:
  "I DON'T WANT TO
  COMMIT..."

LOOK WHERE YOUR
LIFE IS TAKING YOU,

If you feel stuck
in any phase of your
life ... this may be
a   truth

TRUTH

trying to burst forward,
trying to explode,

132

THIS EXPLOSION CAN BE
A NEW BEGINNING,

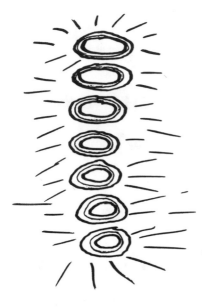

FEEL IT
AND
ALLOW IT

TO COME

FORWARD,
AND
BE EVER SO

THANKFUL

THAT IT IS FINALLY

HAPPENING,

133

FOR WITHOUT THIS
EXPLOSIVE EMOTION
YOU WOULD NEVER
RECOGNIZE A CHANGE
NEEDS TO HAPPEN...

RESPOND
TO
THIS
CHANGE,

Take the next step
and
Commit to finding
your real truths,

Watch how your life
responds around you,

If PEOPLE AROUND you
APPEAR TO BE SPINNING
THEIR WHEELS,

you, too, MAY BE DOING
THE SAME,

136

COMMIT TO OWNING YOUR OWN PROBLEMS,

COMMIT TO FIXING THEM THE BEST WAY YOU KNOW HOW,

COMMIT TO ASKING FOR HELP IF YOU CANNOT FIX THEM YOURSELF,

137

WE EACH HAVE OUR OWN
INDIVIDUAL PATH,
OUR OWN PURPOSE,

COMMITMENT AND
RESPONSIBILITY ARE TWO
VERY IMPORTANT WORDS
IN OUR VOCABULARY,

AND IT IS...

Through our commitment
and our responsibility,
we enable happiness
and prosperity to come
into our lives,

Happiness
comes from within,

It is a gift you give yourself because it is through your commitment and your responsibility that you INVITE HAPPINESS into your being,,,

You have allowed PROSPERITY to be given a form,

140

FOR

HAPPINESS

ATTRACTS

ABUNDANCES,

So

COMMIT...

RESPOND...

BE HAPPY...

AND OPEN YOUR ARMS

WIDE TO THE HEAVENS ABOVE...

FOR YOU SHALL HAVE ALL

THAT IS FOR

THE ASKING!

142

The ABC's for Finding Perfect Love

So many
of us are
desperately
looking
for
perfect
love,

But what is perfect
love?

PERFECT LOVE IS
LOVING YOURSELF
UNCONDITIONALLY WITH
ALL OF YOUR FLAWS,

PERFECT LOVE IS THE
LOVE THAT WILL BRING US
TRUE HAPPINESS,

MANY TIMES WE FAIL
TO LOOK IN THE RIGHT PLACE,

THE PLACE
THAT IS
RIGHT
UNDER OUR NOSES...
OURSELVES!

147

SOMETIMES WE THINK
IT IS EASIER TO GIVE
LOVE TO OTHERS,

BUT HOW CAN WE GIVE
LOVE TO OTHERS BEFORE
WE HAVE
GIVEN LOVE
TO OURSELVES

?

LOVE

148

How can we give a friend a drink of water when the glass is empty and we, too, are thirsty?

When we have learned to fill our own glass and drink from it, then we will be able to give to others,

149

LIKE THE ALPHABET,
WE BEGIN WITH

A B C.

"A," <u>ALWAYS</u> <u>YOU</u> <u>FIRST</u>,

FILL

YOUR

BATHTUB

WITH WARM WATER AND ADD

SOME SEA SALTS OR EPSOM SALTS,

AS YOU POUR THEM IN, SAY

TO YOURSELF "THESE SALTS

WILL HELP ME HEAL MY

WOUNDS,

151

... My emotional, mental, spiritual and physical wounds,"

Get into the water,

Soak your body, your tired muscles, your worried mind, your troubled heart,

LET GO

AND
LET GOD!

LET GOD TAKE THE
PLACE OF EMOTIONS you
HAVE ALLOWED TO WOUND you,

Ask him to supply you with his love or, if that feels scary, ask for love from the universe to come in and fill your vessel

YOUR BODY

WITH LOVE,

As you lie in the bath water, bathe your cells with universal love, with peace of mind, with happiness and joy,

Try to feel these words,

Fill each pore in your entire body with wonderful, positive emotions,

155

TAKE TIME TO BATHE
YOURSELF WITH WONDERFUL
WORDS WHILE YOU BATHE
YOUR BODY IN THE WARM
SALT WATER,

PEACE OF MIND
HAPPINESS
JOY

156

As you lie there
visualize your whole body
being filled with love,

When this happens
your entire vessel, your
body, is filled with
unconditional love ...

ENOUGH TO GIVE
TO OTHERS,

157

"B," BE HAPPY
      BE KIND
        BE JOYFUL
          BE LOVING,

PRACTICE MAKES PERFECT,

PRACTICE GIVING LOVE TO
YOURSELF,

TAP INTO YOUR GOD, YOUR
UNIVERSAL LOVE, AND FILL
YOURSELF UP EVERYDAY,

"C," COMMIT TO LOVING
YOURSELF FIRST AND THEN
PASS ON YOUR LOVE TO OTHERS,

PRACTICE WITH
A WARM SMILE

A KIND GESTURE

A
HELPING
HAND
AND...

159

WHEN YOU FOLLOW THESE
A B Cs
YOUR THIRSTY SOUL
WILL FIND ITS

PERFECT LOVE!!!

A SPECIAL THANKS TO THE MAN WHO HANDED ME THE CARD WITH "RECIPE FOR HAPPINESS",

I LIKED IT SO MUCH I WANTED TO SHARE IT,

161

RECIPE FOR HAPPINESS

TAKE TWO HEAPING CUPS OF
PATIENCE

TWO HANDFULS OF
GENEROSITY

ONE HEARTFUL OF LOVE

DASH OF LAUGHTER

ONE HEADFUL OF
UNDERSTANDING

162

SPRINKLE GENEROUSLY WITH
KINDNESS
ADD PLENTY OF FAITH AND
MIX WELL
SPREAD OVER A LIFETIME
AND SERVE EVERYBODY
YOU MEET!